A Visit to the Zoo

by Rosalyn Clark

BUMBA BOOKS™

LERNER PUBLICATIONS ◆ MINNEAPOLIS

Note to Educators:

Throughout this book, you'll find critical thinking questions. These can be used to engage young readers in thinking critically about the topic and in using the text and photos to do so.

Lerner Publications Company
A division of Lerner Publishing Group, Inc.
241 First Avenue North
Minneapolis, MN 55401 USA

For reading levels and more information, look up this title at www.lernerbooks.com.

Library of Congress Cataloging-in-Publication Data

Names: Clark, Rosalyn, 1990– author.
Title: A visit to the zoo / by Rosalyn Clark.
Description: Minneapolis : Lerner Publications, [2017] | Series: Bumba books. Places we go | Audience: Ages 4–7. | Audience: K to grade 3. | Description based on print version record and CIP data provided by publisher; resource not viewed.
Identifiers: LCCN 2016051012 (print) | LCCN 2016048095 (ebook) | ISBN 9781512450484 (eb pdf) | ISBN 9781512433739 (lb : alk. paper) | ISBN 9781512455663 (pb : alk. paper)
Subjects: LCSH: Zoos—Juvenile literature. | Zoo animals—Juvenile literature.
Classification: LCC QL76 (print) | LCC QL76 .C53 2017 (ebook) | DDC 590.74—dc23

LC record available at https://lccn.loc.gov/2016051012

Manufactured in the United States of America
1 – CG – 7/15/17

LERNER
SOURCE

Expand learning beyond the printed book. Download free, complementary educational resources for this book from our website, www.lernerresource.com.

Table of Contents

Time for a Field Trip

It is time for a field trip.

We are going to the zoo!

There are many animals at the zoo.

Each animal has a different habitat.

We see a panda.

Pandas live in warm habitats.

What other animals live in warm habitats?

We see a polar bear.

Polar bears live in
cold habitats.

They swim in icy cold water.

What other animals live in cold habitats?

Some animals are tall.

A giraffe has a long neck.

It eats leaves from trees.

Some animals are small.

Lemurs sit in trees.

They have striped tails.

Next, we see sea lions.

They swim.

They play together

in the water.

We see more mammals.

Monkeys are mammals.

Monkeys swing from trees.

What other mammals might you see at the zoo?

Then we see reptiles.

Look! There is an alligator!

It has sharp teeth.

There is so much to see

at the zoo!

Would you like to

visit a zoo?

What to See at a Zoo

giraffe

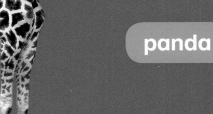

panda

sea lion

polar bear

alligator

Picture Glossary

habitat

the type of place where an animal lives

mammals

animals that have fur and drink milk from their mothers when they are young

reptiles

animals that slither on their bellies or walk on short legs

striped

having different bands of color

23

Read More

Bakowski, Barbara. *A Zany Zoo Day.* Minneapolis: Red Chair Press, 2011.

Ellis, Andy. *When Lulu Went to the Zoo.* Minneapolis: Andersen Press USA, 2008.

Harrison, Sarah. *A Day at a Zoo.* Minneapolis: Millbrook Press, 2009.

Index

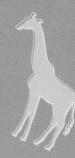

Photo Credits

The images in this book are used with the permission of: © kali9/iStock.com, pp. 4–5; © Hung Chung Chih/Shutterstock.com, pp. 6, 23 (top left); © Bill Grove/iStock.com, pp. 8–9; © BirgerNiss/iStock.com, p. 10; © Henk Bentlage/Shutterstock.com, pp. 13, 23 (bottom right); © Brandon Alms/Shutterstock.com, pp. 14–15; © roejoe/iStockphoto.com, pp. 17, 23 (top right); © Revel Pix LLC/Shutterstock.com, pp. 18, 23 (bottom left); © Dragon Images/Shutterstock.com, pp. 20–21; © jaroslava V/Shutterstock.com, p. 22 (top left); © Eric Isselee/Shutterstock.com, 22 (top right), 22 (bottom right), 22 (bottom middle); © Iakov Filimonov/Shutterstock.com, p. 22 (bottom left).

Front Cover: © kali9/iStock.com.

AUG 2 3 2018